THE WONDERLAND OF HERE AND NOW...

Enjoy Each Day in God's Beautiful World

Written by
Jean Carpenter Welborn

The C.R. Gibson Company
Norwalk, Connecticut

GOD'S WORLD

God's world moves on in calm of faith,
Without a where or why,
Complete, without an utter want—
And of God's world am I!

THE WONDERLAND OF WE

The wonderland of we
Is the gift God gave to me;
His world's design can now be mine:
He gave me eyes to see
His trees and flowers grow
In row on bursting row;
His every bird has sung His word
In splendor, so I'll know
> That where I look, in field or brook,
> In ocean's rise and pounding,
> In season's turn, I seek and learn
> That God is All-surrounding.
The gifts God gives are free
For all to have, for He
Is Author of the book of Love—
"The Wonderland of We."

MY NOW

Not knowing what tomorrow holds in store—
What challenges or blessings, all the more
Should I forego projecting and give up
Tomorrow's cares to drink this moment's cup,
Creatively alive. Life sings, resounds
In harmony with living. Joy abounds.
In meadows nestling into hillside nooks;
In bird flight, swirls of clouds, in chuckling brooks.
It matters not the ground on which I stand,
If I perceive God's miracles at hand
Within this sphere of time in which I thrive,
This eternal moment, free to be alive.
Each one supplies the substance for my plow—
And tomorrows are the harvest of my NOW.

One man esteemeth one day above another; another
esteemeth every day alike. Let every man be
persuaded in his own mind.

Rom. 14:5

THE INFINITE HEART OF GOD

I gazed at the glory of morning, as it spread from an endless sky; at the legion of trees adorning the hills that they fortify. I reveled in birdsongs' sweetness, as it soared through the silver air; and my spirit pulsed with completeness, in knowing that everywhere I looked, without sense of duty, from the sky to the ground I trod, I was seeing beyond to the beauty—the infinite heart of God.

HE GIVES TO US THIS MORNING

As dawn dilutes the night, and heaven's candles dim, a gathering of God chirps forth a morning hymn—crows gladness for the light, joy-tears each grassy blade, swells forth the rose's bud—earth cheers the day, God-made!

Let the heavens be glad, and let the earth rejoice: and let men say among the nations, The Lord reigneth.

I Chron. 16:31

NOW COMES THE HOUR

The hour is come;
The moment is here—
The eternal NOW
Is held in this sphere
Of fullness of time,
Where I can abide
In wide-eyed awareness
That God is my Guide,
Revealing His name
In earth, vine and limb;
Where peace is discovered
In one-ness with Him.

Abide in me, and I in you. As the branch cannot bear fruit of itself, except it abide in the vine; no more can ye, except ye abide in me.

John 15:4

IN
COUNTRY
OR CITY
So often one speeds to the country to seek the true face of God in all Nature's displays—thinking that only the forest, the creek, green fields and wild flowers can sponsor His ways. Back in the city, some think that the crowd—of hurried harried has no time or place—to find Divine proof; that no room is allowed—where God, in the midst of a throng, shows His face. Yet in country or city, wherever one lives, each is God's child, with His kingdom within. Everywhere God loves His children and gives His Spirit to those who claim Him as their kin. In country, open and wide, in city, with avenues broad—both people and places are mirrors of God.

TRUSTED HELP

Since help is my present need,
I would lift up my eyes to the hills.
But flat is the land, and the scene
Is curtained by fog mist that fills
The atmosphere, muffling earth
And its beauty that somewhere abounds.
For even the crash of the surf
Re-echoes in vague, hollow sounds.

Neither seeing nor hearing God's world,
Wherein trusted help ever stood,
At last I seek deep in myself,
And all that I find there is good!
My faith is undaunted, hill-high;
And peace sings an uplifting song.
God's Spirit is radiantly clear:
My help is within me, God-strong!

THE DO-ER

Not once have I been on my knees today.
I have not supplicated God at all.
Instead, while I put laundered clothes away,
I saw His pureness; when I pruned the tall
Rose-bush, His petals velveted my hand;
His water flowed from faucets; and His face
Brightened the sun; and, by His quick command,
The clouds circused the sky with rapid pace.
Down on one's knees, such sights as these slip by
Unseen. Head-up, today I sought to live
And move and have my being, heart and eye,
In God. And I have nothing more to give—
Now that this Truth-discerning day grows dim,
But thankfulness for walking, joyed, with Him.

But be ye doers of the word, and not hearers only,
deceiving your own selves.

James 1:22

ONLY A MOMENT IS NEEDED

I need not travel anywhere
Specific, for my cause,
Since any place is one for prayer
That gives a moment's pause:
A traffic light; a sudden hush
In conversation's stream;
A glance away from work; the brush
Of branch against a beam;—
Now every unsought interlude
I gratefully applaud,
Aware each one has just renewed
My centeredness in God.

THE COMFORTER

Whatever kind of strength we chance to need
Comes comfortingly pouring in, through prayer.
The very turning to our Source is seed
For growing strong is knowing He is there.

GOD'S TENANTS

Whether the land is mountained, rivered, plained, or treed—the splendor contained is fountained to quench our spirits' need. Wherever the land we live in, more glorious it will be, when we realize it has been given—by God for our tenancy.

But the land, whither ye go to possess it, is a land of hills and valleys, and drinketh water of the rain of heaven: A land which the Lord thy God careth for: the eyes of the Lord thy God are always upon it, from the beginning of the year even unto the end of the year.

Deut. 11:11,12

I HOLD THE KEY

My thoughts, at times, are noble, pure, and straight,
Sprung from the fount of Spirit—love that flows
Soul-deep; yet longing to communicate
The prodding touch with Truth that no one knows
Exists in me but God. If thoughts are things,
I cannot rest in halcyon content
With such a treasure pooled in silent springs.
Instead, they beg release; for they are sent,
Divinely ordered, with but one condition:
I turn the key that frees them to fruition.

JUST OPEN THE DOOR

When in my heart there's a place—where I am not totally loving, and so that life seems a riotous race, I know, if I'll only remember, that I can dispel every gloom. For the moment I open the portal, God enters and goldens the room.

THE
PRICELESS
GIFT

This is the day—this golden globe of hours:
A lifetime glows ahead, its hidden powers
Within my grasp to do with as I will—
To scatter fruitlessly or to fulfill
The dreams of yesterday, tomorrow's goals;
And none but me to sight the lurking shoals.
Yet, fearlessly I'll find an open course,
Abetted by past treasures' inner force:
Each failure, each success has given birth
To some significance of future worth.
My eager heart is racing, spirits lift
To meet the challenge of this priceless gift.
I cannot dare ignore finding the way
To live completely—now—this is the day!

*And tomorrow shall be as this day, and much more
abundant.*

Isa. 56:12

HERE AND NOW

This day is different from all other days.
Have you observed the luminescent air?
The pulse of life cupped in the fields' bouquets
Of daisies, swaying with a jaunty flair?
Nor have the cardinals held such confidence
Of cheer, nor have the hollow-throated crows
Cawed quite so lustily on wing and fence,
While even the clouds shape poetry out of prose.
As I recall, those days, tallied as past,
Did not contain the promise waiting here
Around each moment's corner; while the vast
Tomorrows still remain unknown, unclear.
This day is singularly new, somehow—
A sphere of lovely time called "here and now."

*Unto thee lift I up mine eyes, O thou that dwellest
in the heavens.*

Ps. 123:1

ALL IN GOD'S GOOD TIME

God's timing and ours do not always prove to be identical. We moan at blocks, delays, the slowness of fruition of a dream; we stir up frustration, fret our nights and days. We send up prayers, asking that they fly—to heaven, not only for replies to come as *we* prescribe, but also in that time—wherein perfection guides the pendulum. Yet our praying with impatient discontent tethers our pleas. God's time requires release; so He can free His merciful consent—in His right time of goodness, favor, peace. For time acceptable to God is *how* —we give to Him the moment He names NOW.

INWARD LISTENING

As zooming jets flare through the sky,
As rockets roar toward outer space,
As brilliant cars go whizzing by,
This is the time, the day, the place
For inward listening. The sound
Of progress will not change the Voice;
Its message never can be drowned
By outward thunder. Yet the choice
Is ours alone to turn within
To harken to the One true Guide,
Who can be heard despite the din
That rumbles through the world outside.
Quietly, as the stars that glisten,
God speaks, if we will pause and listen.

*Rejoice evermore. Pray without ceasing. In every
thing give thanks: for this is the will of God in Christ
Jesus concerning you. Quench not the Spirit. Prove
all things; hold fast that which is good.*
                                                    I Thes. 5:16-19,21

PROTECTED

There is a shield around me;
I have no cause for fear.
Untouched by hand, unseen by eye,
God's Presence cloaks me here.

Within my body, all about,
God's armor is my guide;
Each forward step I take is sure,
For I take God in stride!

FROM TRIALS...
STRENGTH

When day's events seem like a perfect story of glorious content, of battles won . . . then our humble gratitude flows free, acknowledging how fully blessed are we. In dismal days of trial, there comes temptation to see only our sufferings; we forget that from them comes endurance, our salvation—the pattern whereby character is set. Rejoice, then, in both good and troubled days, secure in God's great Love and wondrous ways.

GOD
WAITS
WITH CARE

Take things to God that may seem hard to bear,
Leave them with Him; take a breath, and rejoice!
Nothing's impossible. God waits with care—
If you will listen, you can hear His voice
Whisper assurance; from His breath of Life,
You will breathe a relief, pure and just.
With each releasing, your faith keeps increasing—
It's God's perfect way that it must.
Take things to God that seem challenges, true;
Leave them with praise! They are burdens no more!
Soft are His hands that build iron-strong trust,
And your heart, light with freedom, will soar.

Thou calledst in trouble, and I delivered thee;

Ps. 81:7

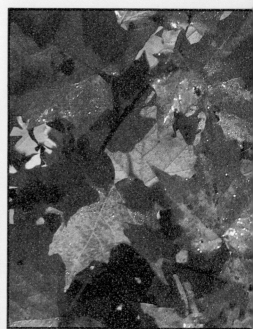

WE CELEBRATE HIS GLORY

The sun in the heavens is warming the land with its radiant rays. And earth in its joy is responding in unique, multitudinous ways. Even cracks in the sidewalk are sprouting—green blades, where a butterfly floats. Hills sing and their echoes come shouting—through currents of crystalline motes. God's glory could never be grander; and trees clap their hands in delight; as we, in bedazzle of wonder, with all His creation unite.

For ye shall go out with joy, and be led forth with peace: the mountains and the hills shall break forth before you into singing, and all the trees of the field shall clap their hands.

Isa. 55:12

WE, THE SEEKERS

Our galaxy is average, we are told. Light years away, whirl others that surpass this one we've come through lenses to behold, and judge more clearly. So, as we amass old boundaries, their limitations fade, and forces once unknown have been revealed. We penetrate the sky and pierce the shade—of ocean depths to reap from nature's field. As barriers melt, the vastness of it all would seem to make a mere speck out of man—a trivial creature—until we recall, these universal findings only can be learned by seeking mortals, ever-awed—sparked by God to disclose His wonderland.

O the depth of the riches both of the wisdom and knowledge of God! how unsearchable are his judgments and his ways past finding out.

Rom. 11:33

MASTER PLAN

How wise was He Who planned the universe,
To keep its myriad secrets so well hidden
From searching minds of men, who would immerse
Their lives to find the key that seems forbidden.
Yet through the bars appear vast hints, then clues
Of revelations, there beyond the seeking.
The challenged cannot now withdraw and lose
A glimpse of final Truth whose Voice is speaking.
And on it goes, this gnawing will to know,
To learn, to solve the secrets, grain by grain.
This striving, too, was planned that we might grow,
From outward in and inward out, with gain.
We cannot then conceive this plan as odd,
If, seeking, we have come heart-close to God.

*Jesus said, "If I have told you earthly things, and ye
believe not, how shall ye believe, if I tell you of
heavenly things?"*

John 3:12

BEING

A rose need not arise each morn to toil throughout the day, or supervise each leaf and thorn, or teach its buds to play, or rearrange its petals so their style is right to see. Regard a rose. It seems to know—it is enough . . . to *be*.

Take, I pray thee, my blessing that is brought to thee;
Gen. 33:11

RENEWAL

There is a sense of certainty in taking—a well-known path where nature dwells supreme—in flowing, ordered change, I can, by seeking at frequent intervals, detect the scheme—the smoothly patterned plan of woodland wonder—as seasons into seasons slowly merge. The promise of it grows as I meander—through homely haunts where dreams again can surge. There is conviction in the white assurance of customary winter. And when green conforms with regulation-spring's appearance, my confidence becomes a buoyant thing. For here the heart's anxieties are stilled, in peace anticipated . . . and fulfilled.

See therefore, and take knowledge of all the lurking places where he hideth himself, and come ye again to me with the certainty.

I Sam. 23:23

I TURN
TO
TRUTH

For, when all my careful, calculated plans
Have, in some sudden disappointing way,
Been rudely halted; when abrupt delay
Stumbled my footsteps with uncalled-for bans
Against my progress, I have come to know
Above all else, this must not cause dismay,
Frustration, anger, thoughts that ricochet
Away from Center, where God's forces flow.
Rather, I turn to Truth and firmly cling.
For, always with my Shepherd as my guide,
I need not feel discouragement inside.
But, opening up my heart, I wait and sing
My thankfulness, because the aftermath
Will find me on my God-appointed path.

I am the good shepherd.

John 10:11

TANGIBLE MOUNTAINS

How fortunate are we who have tangible mountains whose sturdy slopes—stand waiting to receive our gaze, uplifted so to lift our hopes. Their ageless ruggedness confirms God's strength which will not, cannot dim His readiness to share our lives, as we look up and reach to Him. Yet wide the plained horizons stretch, where people plow and pray, then reap. While a city sky is one small patch; yet *there,* God-guided hearts still leap.

For love of God upthrusts from earth, wherever people live who've known—the mountain of far-reaching faith, more lasting than of soil or stone.

THE MIDDLE
OF
THE BRIDGE

I love to be in the middle of the bridge,
The half-way mark where I
Can turn to see where I have been
And muse on going back again,
To the past to identify
Familiar sights, the safe, the sown.
The forward path is strange, unknown,
In a time unlived, on an untouched ridge.
But the middle of the bridge is here—
With its fundamental, present ground;
Where the future and the past must bow
To the infinite, God-way time of NOW.

*Trust in the Lord with all thine heart; and lean not on
thine own understanding. In all thy ways
acknowledge him, and he shall direct thy paths.*
                                                    Prov. 3:5,6

EVEN
IN A
LADYBUG

The ladybug upon my finger,
Having zoomed there, chose to linger,
Then raced across my knuckle, turned,
Sought my nail; then, having learned
All that a finger can reveal,
Took to flight and found my heel.
Its angle was no place to dwell;
She crawled around its curve—and fell
Upside-down, her small feet plinking
Soundless air. But in a twinkling,
One wing extended as a prop,
She flipped an instant upright flop!

Why ladybugs were God-created,
I had not known. 'Til then, elated,
I realized from a wise, red "dot"—
To seek and learn in any spot
You find yourself, though you might fall,
To get right up again is all
That matters. If you take a spill,
You have, within, a greater Will.
So ever fondly I will hug
The memory of that ladybug!

TAKE
TIME TO
SEE

I'd planned a quiet, uneventful day,
A day apart from routine's bee-hive-humming,
In which to shun the commonplace display
About me, with its customary numbing.
I strolled in opalescence through my arbor,
Where infant leaves played hide-and-seek with sun;
Tongued wavelets licked the shoreline of the harbor
As eagerly as if they'd just begun.
A redbird flashed its sudden scintillation
Across the clean and systematic sky;
A bud had popped to flowered animation
Within the fleeting hours since I'd passed by.
And then I knew no day could ever be
Merely routine, if I took time to see.

SHARE EACH MOMENT WITH GOD

There's a time for work and a time for play; time for children and freedom's way. There's reading, learning, digging the sod; but how much time do we give to God? If we pause with Him a moment or two—and think that is all we have time to do—we find ourselves a little blessed, while searching outside for that inner rest. But great would be our hearts' release, in knowing the joy of unwavering peace, if we would seek to link our stride—with God, each moment, as our Guide.

HIS GREATEST
GIFT
God blessed me with hands to work with, with ears to hear, with eyes to view my own horizons of bright or somber skies. A brain to think with purpose motivates each deed, these miracles I prize, but my highest esteem, is for that portion of my being, the citadel of my soul—God's greatest gift to me, the touchstone of all that makes me whole.

But my God shall supply all your need according to his riches in glory by Christ Jesus.

Phil. 4:19

UNITED
IN HIS
LOVE
With varied shapes, a throng of churches stands—and more keep rising (as more spirits cling toward one-ness with their God) across the land—each with its outer creeds that finally bring its people and their hearts to grasp the Hand . . . that shepherds them to His eternal spring.

HARVEST

The grapes are plump on the vine;
The melons are cupped by the ground;
While cherry clumps ruby the trees;
And silver of onions abound.
The cornstalks, tall tepees of tan,
Parade upon fields; squares of hay
Are bundles dropped off in a line
Near pumpkins piled up in display.

With harvest revealing the story,
Each autumn the scenes are the same;
The theme being earth's growing glory,
Whose author has God for its name.

BEYOND WORLDLY RICHES

If I spent wealth as lavishly and generously as Fall is doing now, with coins of gold flung wide for one and all to scamper through and marvel at, I still could not succeed—in causing this quintessence of beauty by my deed.

GOD'S MESSENGERS

When I feel the soft caress of air from distant trees, and sense the fragrance of far flowers, mingling in the breeze; when I hear the fluted notes of birdsong on the wing; or see the sky's soft radiance rainbow an evening; I know these are His messengers, proving constantly, that God in any time and place will come on wings . . . to me.

THE BRIDGE IS FAITH

Bridges wear disguises, for more than spans of steel, cement or wood, their purpose is meaningful and real—in circumstance, in people, ideas, events, and deeds. All these are stepping stones to cross and fill your needs, to grasp at goals of progress. Yet the span most sure, unflawed, is to let your faith in Christ be your one-way bridge to God.

TOMORROW

Tomorrow we'll have one glorious time:
Partners with Nature, far hills we will climb.
Seeking and finding each mark of God's Hand
Touching this parched, undemanding tan land.
Tomorrow we'll trek through the desert and find
Veins of new flowers-of-gold, never-mined,
Touches of green and pale lavendar bloom,
Thrusting through rocks where cracks offered room.
Tomorrow will rainbow so vast an array,
We must be on guard to take heed of today.

The earth is stored in bins of night. Then darkness
works its silent way, depositing, at dawn, the bright
new cornucopia of day.

Take therefore no thought for the morrow, for the
morrow shall take thought for the things of itself.
                                                    Matt. 6:34

But joy cometh in the morning.
                                                    Ps. 30:5

AS CAREFULLY FORMED AS WE

A masterpiece of glistening—this flake, untouched by hand or thing—is intricate in form and plan, and as unique as any man, whose smallest thought is sparked to glow . . . by Him Who forms each flake of snow.

Hast thou entered into the treasures of the snow?
Job 38:22

For he saith to the snow, Be thou on the earth.
Job 37:6

SNOWPRINTS

I watched, late autumn nights and days,
Until the full moon, soft with haze,
Betokened snow. And when at last
White filigree came floating past
My window, eagerly I waited
Until dark earth was white-created.
Then I walked forth, my steps alone
The single sound in a world unknown;
My steps the only proof that I
Returned from touching a snow-starred sky.
By dawn my marks were gone, unhinted;
But on my heart their path is printed.

CIRCLES
OF

LIFE The dimness of the redwood forest floor, leaf carpeted, cone-strewn, sequoias felled by lightning daggers, make perception more alert to froth of fern, green bay trees held by living moss, as sustenance to sprout—their dauntless youth. For everywhere the old aid and encourage new growth thrusting out. Through forest spread the ancient tale is told, of age yielding its strength so youth can be . . . symbolic circle of eternity.

But if the Lord maketh a new thing . . .

Num. 16:30

But if we hope for that we see not, then do we with patience wait for it.

Rom. 8:25

NEW
TO
ME

Perhaps it's true, as I've heard said,
There's nothing new beneath the sun;
And when the cherub lifts his head
To ponder on what should be done
In his New Year, he'll plan to climb
Through space—though further than before;
Find innovations saving time,
New tunes to hum, fresh wealth to store.
Yet if the angles of things new
Are old, made novel by degree,
It will not matter, for their view
Will be breath-taking new to me!

*For by me thy days shall be multiplied, and the years
of thy life shall be increased.*

Prov. 9:11

THE THREAD

I am the thread flowing between the knots of varied size, each one a milestone passed in this, my life; most are minor—small victories that count among the vast.

Yet when Time with her finger starts to roll the final knot to all I'll ever be—then I, my thread, summation of the whole—will flow, unbroken, to infinity.

I know that whatsoever God doeth, it shall be for ever, nothing can be put to it, nor anything taken from it:

Ecc. 3:14

ACKNOWLEDGEMENTS

The author and publisher have made every effort to trace and acknowledge the publications in which some of the poems in this volume were originally published. In the event of any question arising as to the use of such material, the publisher, while expressing regret for inadvertent error, will be pleased to make the necessary corrections in future printings. Thanks are due to the following publications for permission to use the poems indicated.

CHRISTIAN HOME, April 1958, "Center of All" ("His Greatest Gift") copyright © 1958; January 1959, "New" ("New to Me") copyright © 1959 The Methodist Publishing House.

CHURCH SCHOOL, 1965, "Scientific Report" ("We, the Seekers") copyright © 1965 The Methodist Publishing House.

CONQUEST, June 1956, "The Necessary Time" ("Share Each Moment With God"); August 1956, "Song for Every Day" ("From Trials . . . Strength"); May 1957, "The Sight Beyond" ("The Infinite Heart of God").

EXTENSION MAGAZINE, July 1958, "Master Plan."

IMPROVEMENT ERA, May 1956, "Spring Morning" (Take Time to See").

LIFE AND HEALTH, September 1967, "Of Certainty" ("Renewal"); February 1958, "Snowflake" ("As Carefully Formed as We").

THE NEW YORK TIMES, September 1956, "The Thread" copyright ©1956 by the New York Times Company.

THE WAR CRY, July 1958, "Inward Listening."

THE WASHINGTON EVENING STAR, January 1957, "The Priceless Gift."

THE YOUTH'S INSTRUCTOR, September 1963, "This Day" ("Here and Now"); 1965, "Essence" ("Being"); January 1961, "Snowprints."

Type set in Optima
Designed by Karen Murphy-Pokluda

Photo Credits

Four By Five, Inc.—cover, pp.23, 38; Jim Patrick—cover; Michael Powers—cover; Pat Powers—cover, p.27; Lois Bowen—p.2; Klauss Brahmst—p.6; Carl Moreus—p.10; Wyoming Travel Commission—p.15; James Power—p.15; Gene Ruestmann—pp.15, 19, 23, 35; State of Vermont—pp.23, 30, 47; Three Lions, Inc.—p.30; Lee Whittles—p.30; Janet Nelson—p.38; Jacqueline Marsall—pp.38, 55; Maria Demarest—p.42; Eric Sanford—p.47; Bruce Ando—pp.47, 51; Jay Johnson, p.55.